D0926181

CONTENTS

ACKNOWLEGMENTS

Big Spring, Texas was home to two military training bases, which produced some of the finest pilots in the world. The bases contributed to the growth and development of Howard County by providing jobs for thousands of residents and by pumping millions into the local economy. The loss of Webb AFB left a void that could never be filled. I want to thank the United States Air Force for donating the photographs (taken at Webb), to the museum. These photographs provide glimpses of everyday life, key figures, and significant events that shaped the Bombardier School and Webb.

I would like to thank Jerry and Katie Grimes for the information and photographs they provided for this book. A special thank you goes to Peter Bird, who loaned photographs he took while training as a pilot at Webb. I owe a debt of gratitude to The Big Spring Herald, Joe Pickle, and all the writers who wrote articles on the Bombardier School and Webb AFB through the years. These recorded articles have become invaluable research material.

Last but certainly not least, I want to thank Nancy Raney and Beth Purcell for their hard work and encouragement.

I dedicate this book to the people who served at Webb AFB and The Big Spring Bombardier School. From Brigadier General to Civil Service Clerk, I hope this book evokes good memories of the times they spent at The Bombardier School or Webb, and in Howard County.

Finally I dedicate this book in memory of the men and women who have lost their lives while protecting and defending our rights to freedom.

INTRODUCTION

For two years, before the bombing of Pearl Harbor, plans had been underway for an Army flying school to be located in Big Spring. However, soon after the surprise attack by the Japanese, the need for these schools became evident and they began to formulate all over the United States. On April 2, 1942, it was announced that the Army Air Force would activate schools in Big Spring, Midland and San Angelo to train bombers. Col. Sam L. Ellis was immediately assigned to the new bombardier school as project officer, and later designated at Commanding Officer.

The city of Big Spring quickly passed $100,000 in bonds for purchase of additional land adjoining the municipal airport west of town. Utility companies worked on extending service, roads were cleared, and by mid-May, construction was underway, with over 300 units from the United States Corps of Engineers involved in the base's construction. Laborers with little carpentry skills were recruited into service in order to rush completion. The base was still far from completion, when the first troops arrived early to set up for the trainees. Tar-paper covered buildings awaited them as the troops quickly joined in on the building process. Gasoline transports and other equipment arrived, as well as trainer planes, which were rolled onto a huge apron at the school.

On September 25, 1942, the "Four Month Miracle" was ready for the first cadet's arrival. The new class of bombardiers arrived from 30 states to the Big Spring Army Air Force Advanced Flying School. Among the young men were a steel worker, polo player, romance language translator, a Montana cowboy, and a police officer. Lt. Col. John W. White, director of training, repeatedly called for the "aggressive spirit and to be

prepared for the bloody business of war." Col.
White said, "Toil and sweat are ahead, and
training will be long and arduous; but when they
are completed, twelve weeks hence, this first
class of bombardiers from the Big Spring School
will be among the finest fighters in the world."
Captain Bradstreet administered the bombardier's
oath to the class. The oath bound them to defend
their country to their death and to protect to
their death, the secret of America's bombsights.
The 12-week course consisted of four three-week
periods. Starting with ground school, air
training, "refinement" technique, and simulated
combat bombing. Upon graduation, the bombardier
student was commissioned second lieutenant in the
United States Army Air Force and awarded the
silver "wings" of the bombardiers.

Exactly one year and 10 days after the
Japanese struck Pearl Harbor, the first class of
118 young men graduated. Rep. George Mahon,
chairman of the House sub-committee on military
expenditures, addressed the newly commissioned
Second Lieutenants during the ceremony.   Rep.
Mahon reminded the young bombardiers that they
were on a mission of good - a mission to destroy
evil. He said this was an honorable task, and it
was their chance to do something about ridding
the world of a deadly infection. Air power
carried the message of hope for this country. He
added there was no doubt about the final issue of
the war."

In 1945, the school produced student
bombardiers from four nations, including the
United States, France, Brazil, and China. The
last graduating class from this school was
composed entirely of Chinese students. Over 3000
military personnel and several hundred civilians
worked at the bombardier base. At the end of
World War II, Big Spring Bombardier School was
deactivated and was then used as a municipal
airport.

The Korean crisis once again disturbed
America's peace, and in 1951, the

Air Force Base's 3560th Pilot Training Wing was reactivated. As a "thank you" gesture, the city of Big Spring deeded 1,247 acres to Webb, with an additional 1200 acres leased for $1 a year. The base was opened on October 1, 1951, and Col. Ernest F. Wackwitz Jr. was named Webb's first Base Commander. On May 19, 1952, Webb had its official open house to announce its mission as a jet single engine pilot training station.

The first class of pilot trainees arrived on March 26, 1952. Graduation date for the class of 52-D was on June 20, 1952, at which time the aviation cadets received their diplomas and silver wings, and were commissioned Second Lieutenants.

In April 1952, five on-base houses were built and three hundred rent homes in Big Spring's Monticello addition were made available before the Capehart on-base housing was built in 1958.

The base was dedicated and renamed on May 18, 1952, for Lt. James L. Webb Jr., a Big Spring pilot who was killed off the coast of Japan on June 16, 1949.

Once Webb AFB was activated, student jet pilots trained in the propeller driven T-28 Trojan and the T-33 T-Bird jet. During early 1956, the propeller driven aircraft was fazed out of the program, leaving the pilots the T-33 jets for training. In 1960, the base received the Cessna T-37 trainers, and began training in the Northrop T-38 Talon in 1961. In January 1963, the last T-33 was phased out of the Air Force Base program.

From August 1958 to 1967, an important part of Webb was the Air Defense Command. The 331st Fighter Interceptor Squadron arrived from New York and was moved onto the west side of the base. During their nine years at Webb, the 331st pilots flew F-86's, F-102's and F-104's.

A Rescue detachment was also prominent in Webb's history. The unit was first equipped with H-21 helicopters, and later graduated to HH-43B

Huskies shortly before they departed Webb in
1973.
During Webb's history over 10,000 Air Force
pilots graduated and earned their silver wings.
     In addition to honoring fallen pilot Lt.
James Webb, Webb AFB dedicated the newly
constructed academics building to the late Brig
Gen. Howard J. Withycombe. Gen. Withycombe was
Base Commander and had been recently named Brig.
General, when he was involved in a deadly
automobile accident on January 5, 1964. On
August 3, 1975, the base's new dining hall was
dedicated to Capt. Steven L. Bennett, a former
Webb student and recipient of the Medal of Honor.
Capt. Bennett was killed on June 22, 1972, when
his plane crashed into the Gulf of Ton kin. The
Recreation Center was dedicated to the memory of
Sergeant John H. Lees, a local Big Spring
resident who lost his life during World War II.
In 1963 a Chapel Memorial Window Fund was
established to honor those who had lost their
lives and who had served in the pilot training
program at Webb as well as a tribute to the
living. The beautiful stain glass window was
located at the Base chapel.
     By 1970, Webb pumped more than a million
dollars monthly into Big Spring's economy. Over
27,000,000 gallons of JP-4 fuel was purchased
from Cosden Oil & Chemical Co. Utilities (gas,
water, electricity) totaled more than $300,000 a
month. Military personnel alone spent over a
million dollars annually for housing. Salaries
were another major contributing factor in Big
Spring's economy with over
$24,000,000 earned in 1970 by 700 civilian
employees and 2,245 military personnel. Webb
also spent over a million dollars in the purchase
of local goods and services.
     Construction began on the $2.5 million
dormitories in 1975 and funding was approved for
a new theater and officer's dormitory.   January
1976, Senator John Tower answered rumors of
Webb's immanent closure by saying "the future of
Webb is up to Congress."   Local residents were

urged to write letters to President Ford
protesting the closing of Webb.   Unfortunately
their efforts were futile, On March 30, 1977, the
head lines in the Big Spring Herald cries, "Long
battle ends, Webb dies."   Webb personnel started
receiving assignments to other bases and by
October 1977, the base had been reduced to a
caretaker force
of 350 before it's final closure.   An era ended
when Webb presented wings to the last students to
graduate from Webb Air Force Base in December
1975.   The 10,422nd U.S. pilot to graduate was
Capt. Dent. W. Young.   A perfect marriage between
community and base was now over and Big Spring
residents mourned the loss of an old friend.

ONE

BIG SPRING BOMBARDIER SCHOOL

The wide-open West Texas plains offered plenty of range for target practice for the young bombardier students. On October 19, 1942, the first 100-pound practice bomb was dropped by a former collegiate and professional football player, First Cadet Arthur H. Ditt. Joining Ditt on the first practice run was Instructor, Lt. William L. Derling and Second Cadet Frank E. Arnold.

Col. Sam L. Ellis. Col. Sam L. Ellis was first assigned as project officer at the Big Spring Bombardier School. The reserved, yet friendly officer from Tennessee became the first commanding officer when headquarters was activated June 28, 1942. Col. Ellis died suddenly of a heart attack on March 8, 1943. (Bradshaw Collection, Heritage Museum.)

Students Arrival. Bombardier students arrived in Big Spring by train. The West Texas heat and blowing sand was a startling surprise to many. (U.S.A.F. Collection, Heritage Museum.)

Roll Call. After de-boarding the train, students lined up for roll call, grabbed their barrack bags, and were transported to the base in Army trucks. Upon arrival at the Bombardier base, students were disappointed to find their new quarters consisted of tarpaper shacks and outdoor latrines. (U.S.A.F. Collection, Heritage Museum.)

Five-Ship Formations. A five-ship formation of At-11 bombers thunder their way over Big Spring. (Worthy Collection, Heritage Museum.)

Bulls-Eye. R.T. Tollett and C.T. McLaughlin watch on horseback at the north slope of Scenic Mountain as the Bombardiers practice their target. The Big Spring Bombardier School got permission to install this 30-ft. circle as the bulls-eye when it hosted the first bombing Olympics in the late summer of 1943. As the first year of the Bombardier school came to an end so did the target practice. The Army viewed this maneuver as wasteful and a needless exercise, and ordered it suspended. (Bradshaw Collection, Heritage Museum.)

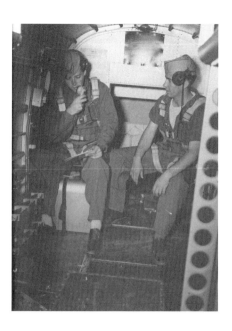

Bombing Missions. Target bombing missions would start at the
"uncivilized" hour of five a.m. A short briefing would take
place before crowding into the compact space of the propeller
driven AT-11.   The pilot would gather his information
including readings of temperature, airspeed, and altitudes
before the bomb bays would be manually opened. Once the plane
reached ten thousand feet, the instructor would signal for the
bombing to begin. The new pilot would have to work fast with
impeccable accuracy.   (Heritage Museum.)

Three-Ship Formation. These AT-11s are in a "three-ship formation" flying high over Big Spring. The AT-11 Kansan could speed at 215 miles per hour, and soar to 20,000 feet with a range of 850 miles. The AT-11 was used during World War II to train the Bombardiers. (Heritage Museum.)

Bombardier Students. The Big Spring Bombardier School graduated its first class of 118 bombardiers one year and 10 days after the Japanese bombed Pearl Harbor. Ground school had to be completed before a pilot could reach for the sky. (Heritage Museum.)

15

The Norden. The Norden Bombsight, invented by Carl Lucas Norden, was an extremely accurate instrument used to guide a bomb to its target. The Mark XV bombsight was a gyro-stabilized device originally commissioned by the U.S. Navy. It was loosely said that by using the device, the bombs could be dropped from 10,000 feet into a pickle barrel. In truth the accuracy and precision was largely in the hands of the bombardier and the information that was fed into the computer instrument. The Norden instruments were stored in a heavily guarded vault and when students prepared for practice runs, they had to get special clearance into the vaulted area. The students would exit the plane and carry the device in pairs while the other two bombardiers followed with their pistols drawn. At the end of World War II, security lessened as many of the boxes had fallen into enemy hands resulting from downed aircraft. (Big Spring Herald Collection, Heritage Museum.)

W.A.A.C. On June 12, 1943, arrival of 14 women of the Woman's Army Auxiliary Corps, created excitement among the men at the Bombardier school. The WAACs participated in community functions and furnished entertainment for the students. They also performed office work and other duties, which allowed the servicemen to complete other assignments. (Heritage Museum.)

Bombs. In 1942, an unidentified "bomb handler" at the Big Spring Bombardier school, holds a practice bomb. The Target bombs were made of metal shells, which had to be fused and loaded with five pounds of powder to produce enough smoke for photographing during target practice. Then 83 pounds of sand was added into the casing to simulate the weight of a real bomb. Big Spring Herald Collection, Heritage Museum.)

Bombardier Flight Line. Propeller driven AT-11s are lined up on the flight line and the bombs are in position for loading onto the planes. (U.S.A.F. Collection, Heritage Museum.)

"Chow Time." A cook serves "chow" to hungry cadets in the mess hall. Tired students found the food became more appetizing as their training progressed. On a typical day, some of the base consumptions were: 2,500 pounds of potatoes, 650 quarts of milk, 700 loaves of bread, 5,000 eggs, and 300 gallons of coffee. (U.S.A.F. Collection, Heritage Museum.)

French Squadron. The French Squadron upon graduation at the Big Spring Bombardier School. (Cox Collection, Heritage Museum.)

Dance at Settles. Students and dance partners enjoy a social evening at the Settles Hotel Ballroom. In 1942, the city's first USO served sandwiches and refreshments to the local Bombardier students, as well as to thousands of troops traveling through Big Spring on the Texas and Pacific railroad. The junior volunteers helped at the USO by serving as game and dance partners. They had to abide by strict guidelines, such as, being invited to join the USO, pledge not to leave the dance floor during dances, come and depart only with their adult sponsor, and use no intoxicants. (U.S.A.F. Collection, Heritage Museum.)

Shine Philips. Shine Philips took the students from the Bombardier school, and later Webb's foreign students, under his wing. The soldiers and WAACs enjoyed Shine's sodas as well as his homespun philosophy. The Main Street drug store was a favorite hangout for civilians as well. (Heritage Museum.)

Graduation. After completing eighteen weeks of Bombardier school, the cadets are sad to say goodbye to Big Spring, but eager to fly the skies and do their patriotic duty. (U.S.A.F. Collection, Heritage Museum.)

Jeep Rides. On the first anniversary of the bombing of Pearl Harbor, a large rally was held by the Bombardier school troops. Jeep rides were given to all who purchased a bomb. (Kesterson Collection, Heritage Museum.)

Rally. The 315th AAF band, along with a small force from the Texas Defense Guard and the Civil Air Patrol, led the Bombardier School troops. The May Rally parade marches west on Third Street. (Kesterson Collection, Heritage Museum.)

22

Successful Day. It was announced that the city sold $85,000 in bonds in the single day bomb-bond rally. Howard County sold $2,000,000 in bonds during the first year anniversary of the attack on America. (Kesterson Collection, Heritage Museum.)

Talented Bands. With the many talents of the Bombardier students, musicals and concerts were performed often in Big Spring. (Heritage Museum.)

Briefing. These students were being briefed before their practice-bombing mission. Targets were located 50 to 75 miles away from the base. Bombardiers practiced dropping bombs from different heights, during the daylight hours as well as at night. Bombardier students paired up, taking turns dropping bombs and operating the camera. (Heritage Museum.)

Bombs Would Be Worse. Willard Sullivan did not miss a chance to advertise the sale of defense stamps after high winds broke the window of Sullivan's drug store. (Bradshaw Collection, Heritage Museum.)

U.S. War Bonds. A young couple purchase U.S.War Bonds before entering the theatre. (Heritage Museum)

TWO
WEBB AIR FORCE BASE

By 1976, Webb had over $128 million worth of facilities and a payroll of more than $33 million per year, which had a tremendous impact on the economy of Big Spring. The base continued to build and grow until the closure date was announced.

James L. Webb.   Lt. James L. Webb Jr. was born July 20, 1924. He and his family moved to Big Spring in 1928 where he attended Big Spring schools. After graduating from high school, he entered the University of Texas as a cadet at Foster Field. Lt. Webb met Doris Taylor at the university, and was married following Lt. Webb's graduation from pilot training school in 1944. The couple had two children, Karen and James Jr. before Lt. Webb was assigned to a fighter group in Europe, in January 1945. He went on to complete 49 combat missions in the European theater of operations in World War II, before being redeployed to Japan. He returned to the United States at the end of World War II, and was discharged from active duty in 1945. In 1948, Lt. Webb returned to the Air Force, and was once again assigned to Japan. On June 16, 1949, while on a weather mission off the coast of Japan, his P-51 Mustang went out of control and plummeted into the bay. On May 18, 1952, Webb Air Force Base was officially dedicated to his memory. (U.S.A.F. Collection, Heritage Museum.)

Dedication. On May 16, 1962, a dedication plaque was placed at Webb Air Force Base honoring Lt. James L. Webb Jr. His mother Mrs. Rilla Webb, who was employed at both the Big Spring Bombardier School and at Webb AFB, was present for the dedication. Mrs. Webb stands beside Col. Wilson Banks, Commander of Webb AFB from August 19, 1961 until July 8, 1963. (U.S.A.F. Collection, Heritage Museum.)

Capehart Housing. On January 22, 1958, an official groundbreaking ceremony of the Capehart housing division at Webb Air Force Base was held. Left to right are: Maj. Gen. Henry R. Spicer, Chief of Staff for the Air Training Command Col. Charles Young, and Col. Kyle L. Riddle. (U.S.A.F. Collection, Heritage Museum.)

View Of Housing. In 1958, Webb's new Capehart Housing area
was already showing signs of progress. The area had been
cleared of brush and leveled with rows of piled drainage pipe
dotting the area. The northerly shot was made from a Webb
helicopter on the south boundary of the housing. (U.S.A.F.
Collection, Heritage Museum.)

Home Life. 460 homes were built in the Capehart housing area
at Webb. The units ranged from 2 to 4 bedrooms and were ready
to move into by the beginning of 1959. (U.S.A.F. Collection,
Heritage Museum.)

Salute. A student pilot returns a salute as he enters Webb's main gate. (U.S.A.F. Collection, Heritage Museum.)

Base Hospital. In 1969, the hospital and dental services
were no longer housed in separate locations but combined in a
new modern medical facility, which provided aero medical
support and physiological training to the Wing Flying Training
Mission. The facility also offered specialties in pediatrics,
internal medicine and general surgery. (U.S.A.F. Collection,
Heritage Museum.)

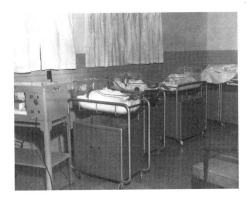

Hospital Nursery. The nursery at Webb's base hospital was
kept busy with the new arrivals. (U.S.A.F. Collection,
Heritage Museum.)

John H. Lees Service Center. On May 20, 1960, a ceremony was held dedicating the Recreation Service Center to the memory of Sergeant John H. Lees, a Texas resident who was killed in China during World War II.

Service Center. In 1956, the John H. Lees Service Club was dedicated and remodeled with, a portrait of the Sergeant hanging in the main ballroom. The service club was a meeting place for Webb servicemen and their families. The center offered participation in many different games such as ping-pong, shuffleboard, billiards, checkers, etc. It also provided five Sunday newspapers, morning coffee, stereos, a photo hobby room, musical instruments, TV viewing, a lounge area, and a kitchen for snacks. (U.S.A.F. Collection, Heritage Museum.)

Dining Hall. The Webb Dining Hall provided hot meals for airmen. A new modern facility was built in 1975 and dedicated to Capt. Steven L. Bennett. (U.S.A.F. Collection, Heritage Museum.)

Commissary. The Commissary sold merchandise at cost with a small surcharge. They carried canned goods, bakery items, frozen foods, meats, produce, health, beauty aids and cigarettes. The "box boys" bagged and carried out the merchandise in exchange for a small tip from the customer. (U.S.A.F. Collection, Heritage Museum.)

Base Exchange. The Base Exchange's main retail outlet carried
lines of civilian clothing as well as military clothing.
Tobacco products, toilet articles, household goods and many
other items could be purchased at the Base Exchange. The BX
consisted of the main retail outlet, Four Seasons store,
Flight Line Cafeteria, a service station, Prairie Pantry and
the Laundromat. Other concessions included a tailor shop,
optical shop, cleaners, beauty and barber shops, located at
various locations around the base. (U.S.A.F. Collection,
Heritage Museum.)

Service Station. The Base Exchange Service Station was located west of the east gate. (U.S.A.F. Collection, Heritage Museum.)

Car Wash. By 1959, Webb had provided airmen and officers with a "Do It Yourself Auto Wash Rack". (U.S.A.F. Collection, Heritage Museum.)

Officers Club. The Officer's Open Mess provided lunch and dinner services as well as bridge, buffets, coffees, teas, cocktail parties and pool parties. Well-known artists and dinner theatre productions provided weekly entertainment, including dances, rock bands, and occasional floorshows. Memberships were open to officers and their dependents. (U.S.A.F. Collection, Heritage Museum.)

Officers Pool. The Officer's Open Mess pool was open to all Officer members and their guests. The pool was one of three that was located at Webb. (U.S.A.F. Collection, Heritage Museum.)

Withycombe Hall. Withycombe Hall was dedicated on March 31, 1964, in honor of Brig. Gen. Howard J. Withycombe, Commander of the 3560th Pilot Training Wing. Withycombe Hall was the sight for classroom instruction for the student pilots training at Webb. On July 5, 1964, 48-year-old General Withycombe who served as Wing Commander at Webb for less than a year was killed in a car wreck east of Big Spring. (U.S.A.F. Collection, Heritage Museum.)

N.C.O. Club. The N.C.O. Club had memberships open to airmen first class and all non-commissioned officers assigned to Webb. It was the center of base social life and included a large ballroom, dining room, cocktail lounge, and a combined game room with a well stocked bar. Dances and bands were regular features along with family game nights and bingo.
(U.S.A.F. Collection, Heritage Museum.)

Theatre. Webb's movie theatre was equipped with upholstered seats, cinemascope screen and a concession bar. First run and classic motion picture productions on the Army-Air Force Motion Picture circuit were shown nightly.
(U.S.A.F. Collection, Heritage Museum.)

Hobby Shop. Many hobby shops were available to Webb personnel.With such diversified interests in woodwork, ceramics, photography,and automobiles. The Auto Hobby Shop offered facilities for the "do it yourself mechanic". It had seven work stalls, a lube rack, a machine area, welding shop and auto storage area.The charge was 25 cents per hour with a maximum of $1 per day for any type work being done in the shop. (U.S.A.F. Collection, Heritage Museum.)

Supply. The supply system was responsible for requisition, receiving, storage, and issuing varied items throughout the airbase. Approximately seven officers, 250 airmen, and 90 civilians worked in supply. (U.S.A.F. Collection, Heritage Museum.)

Control Tower. Student pilots of the 3560th Pilot Training Wing made hundreds of takeoffs and landings daily. The highly trained Air Traffic Controllers assigned to the 2050th Communications Squadron monitored them from the control towers. (U.S.A.F. Collection, Heritage Museum.)

The T-41A. Instructors pose in front of the propeller driven T-41A, which was used for beginning students at Webb. The small plane is comparable to the Cessna 172. It had a speed of 138 miles per hour, and a range of 720 miles with a ceiling of 10,000 feet. (U.S.A.F. Collection, Heritage Museum.)

Base Guard house. The mission of the military police division at Webb was to provide law enforcement and security support for the base. (U.S.A.F. Collection, Heritage Museum.)

Radar. The radarscope controlled airborne traffic. In 1967, the radar facility (GPN-12) was one of the most modern units in operation. (U.S.A.F. Collection, Heritage Museum.)

Base Operations. Base Operations processed passengers, aircrew, flight plans and clearances. It was the focal point for the arrival of visitors and often called the "Gateway to the Air Base." The center also housed the communications center that linked the control towers, flight service stations and air traffic control centers. The 24th Weather Squadron, a division of the Military Airlift Command, operated the weather station. Weather radar and remote controlled meteorological calibration equipment was located between the runways and collected weather data. (U.S.A.F. Collection, Heritage Museum.)

Webb's Chapel. Services marking the opening of Webb Air Force Base Chapel were held Sunday, August 22, 1954. The religious program was designed to provide opportunities for all faiths to worship at the chapel. (U.S.A.F. Collection, Heritage Museum.)

Chapel Memorial Window. In 1963, a Chapel Memorial Window
Fund was established. The window was a memorial tribute to
all who lost their lives while serving in Webb's Pilot
Training Mission, and as a tribute to the living. Lt. Lance
C. Faust, a student at Webb, designed the 10 By 15 foot
window. A beautiful description of the stained glass was
written by a writer in the (Prairie Pilot), " God is depicted,
by a colorful burst of light rays piercing the universe and
spotlighting the world held within the hand of God, and
shining also upon a U.S. Air Force emblem and upon vehicles of
flight, symbolic of the part played in world peace by the Air
Force. A streamer at the bottom is inscribed: 'WHO GUARD THE
PEACE.' The window is now located at the Hangar 25 Air Museum
in Big Spring, Texas. (Heritage Museum.)

THREE
READY TO SERVE

Many officers, pilots and airmen left this small town, only to go to horrific conditions and to lands unknown, to fight in bloody battles that will be etched in their minds forever. We must never forget the sacrifices that were made by millions of Americans who went to war for our freedom.

Jet Ride. Five men from Big Spring, prepare for a ride in an Air Force jet at Webb. Left to right are: Bill Hensley, Dr. John Hogun, Dan Crosley, Leroy Tidwell, and Jimmy Beal. (Hogun Collection, Heritage Museum.)

Interceptor Squadron. Airmen from Stewart Air Force Base in New York wish 2nd Lt. David Maneilly luck on his flight to his new post at Webb Air Force Base. Thirteen pilots of the 331st, led by their commanding officer, Lt. Col. Richard C. Watson, were sent to Webb Air Force Base on Monday August 2, 1958, to serve under the Interceptor Squadron and Air Defense Command. It became the 1247th Combat Training Squadron shortly before it's deactivation in 1967. (U.S.A.F. Collection, Heritage Museum.)

Arrival At Webb. Webb AFB Commander Col. Kyle L. Riddle, (left) and Col. John T. Fitzwater (center) greet Lt. Col. Richard C. Watson, Commander of the 331st Fighter Interceptor Squadron, upon his arrival at Webb from Newburgh, New York. (U.S.A.F. Collection, Heritage Museum.)

45

Wackwitz. Col. Wackwitz served at Webb from October 1, 1951 to July 16, 1953.He was the first to assume command of the new3560th Pilot Training Wing when it was activated in August 1951.He made the old World War II installation operable and Habitable by getting the flying training program into action. (U.S.A.F. Collection, Heritage Museum.)

Maddux. Lt. Gen. Sam Maddux speaks at the podium during Webb's 25[th]anniversary.In 1967, Lt. Gen. Maddoux was commander of the Air Training Command, with its headquarters located at Randolph AFB.(U.S.A.F. Collection, Heritage Museum)

Withycombe. General Withycombe was notified of his nomination to the grade of Brigadier General during his first week of command at Webb. The 48-year-old California native held the position of Wing Commander from July 29, 1963 to the time of his death on Jan. 5, 1964. The General was a Command Pilot with more than 5,000 hours of flying time. (U.S.A.F. Collection, Heritage Museum.)

Withycombe Funeral. In top photo, Lt. Gen. William S. Stone marches with Airmen during General Withycomb's memorial services. Gen. Withycomb's death brought sorrow to Big Spring residents as well as Webb A.F.B. He was active in many community activities including little league, Boy Scouts, and the Rotary Club. General Withycombe had been confirmed Brigadier General on November 1, 1963, two months before his death. (U.S.A.F. Collection, Heritage Museum.)

Peter Bird. Second Lieutenant
Peter Bird graduated on October
26, 1968, at Webb AFB. The "Tiger"
photograph was taken of every
UPT student prior to graduation.
(Courtesy of Peter Bird.)

Gen. Sam Maddux Jr. Lt. Gen.
Sam Maddux Jr. (left), Commander
of the U.S.A.F. Air Training
Command, was given royal treatment
as he arrived at Webb A.F.B. for
Webb's 25th Anniversary Ceremonies.
Lt. Gen. Maddux is welcomed by the
Ambassador's Club of the Big Spring
Chamber of Commerce and Col. Chester
J. Butcher (right) Wing Commander
of Webb in 1967. (U.S.A.F.
Collection, Heritage Museum.)

Foreign Students Graduate. Lt. General Sam Maddux Jr. (left), and Col. Chester Butcher, pin medals onto graduating foreign students at Webb in 1967. (U.S.A.F. Collection, Heritage Museum.)

Welcoming Col. Fred Dean. Bob Whipkey (left) and Ralph Gossett (right) welcome Gen Fred M. Dean back to Webb on Webb's 25th Anniversary. Gen. Dean was the second Base Wing Commander at Webb, serving from July 19, 1953 through November 20, 1954. (U.S.A.F. Collection, Heritage Museum.)

Col. Lauer. Col. Lauer, with the Family Services Program, presents an orientation folder to a Webb dependent. (U.S.A.F. Collection, Heritage Museum.)

Seventh Birthday Coffee. Maj. Gen. H.K. Mooney, Vice Commander of the Air Training Command, presents a certificate on May 8, 1964 to Norma Kuhn's, Supervisor of Family Services. Family Services was organized to help alleviate or solve personal problems of Air Force personnel and their dependents. (U.S.A.F. Collection, Heritage Museum.)

Coffee Table. Family Service ladies provide a coffee table
for an orientation course. The course provided Air Force
families with important information regarding their personal
affairs. Left to right are: Mrs. Charles Head, Mrs. Charles
Dorsey, Mrs. Marshall Kuhns, and Mrs. John Bartlett.
(U.S.A.F. Collection, Heritage Museum.)

Hospital Mural. Volunteers with Family Services designed a
mural for the pediatric waiting room of the 3560th Air Force
Hospital. The mural was designed to "attract and distract
children" while they waited to see the pediatrician. Mrs.
Edwin J. Emmons (left) is shown with Dr. Francis N. Medici and
an unidentified child. (U.S.A.F. Collection, Heritage
Museum.)

Lt. General Dean Speaks. After leaving Webb in 1954, Col. Dean advanced to Lt. General. He served as director of operations to the Joint Chiefs of Staff in Washington, Deputy Commander, then Commander of the 12th Air Force and Assistant Director of the Arms Control and Disarmament Agency in Washington. Concurrent with his assignment with the Strike Command, he served as Deputy Commander in Chief for U.S. defense activities in the Middle East, Southern Asia, and Africa, (south of the Sahara). (U.S.A.F. Collection, Heritage Museum.)

Communications Squadron. The 2050th Communications Squadron was a unit of Webb Air Force Base Communications Service. The Squadron provided the base with base communications, continental and intercontinental communications as well as navigational aids, air traffic control and emergency mission support. A new RAPCON control area updated the older radar controls. (U.S.A.F. Collection, Heritage Museum.)

Major Gray.   Major Gray retired from Webb in 1969 after 26
years of Air Force Service. He was a pilot during World War
II logging more than 5,500 hours of flying time. Between
wars, Major Gray received a Bachelor of Science degree in
Agricultural Economics. He was brought back to active duty
during the Korean War where he flew the L-5 and L-20 liaison
aircraft. Major Gray arrived at Webb in time to receive the
Air Medal with three oak leaf clusters. In 1964, he was
selected one of the outstanding supply officers in the Air
Force. (U.S.A.F. Collection, Heritage Museum.)

Jet Engines. Major Richard A. Gray, Chief of Academics, is explaining the mechanisms of a jet engine to Col. Chester Butcher (left), and the Jordanian Chief of Staff (center). (U.S.A.F. Collection, Heritage Museum.)

Aerodynamics Classroom. Colonel
Chester Butcher gives a tour
of the Aerodynamics classroom,
to the Jordanian Chief of Staff.
Lt. Cook (left) explains the
principals of flight.
(U.S.A.F. Collection,
Heritage Museum.)

Award Presented. Colonel
Sherwood presents Donna Riegel
with a charm and bracelet for
80 hours of volunteer service
with Family Services.
(U.S.A.F. Collection,
Heritage Museum.)

Volunteers. During the summer of 1965, Mrs. A.F. Taute and her daughter, Anette, volunteer with Family services. (U.S.A.F. Collection, Heritage Museum.)

Carmichael. Capt. Thomas O. Carmichael was Weather Instructor in the academic section at Webb. He was named Classroom Instructor of the quarter for three consecutive months in 1968. In addition to his instructor duties, Captain Carmichael served as Academic Test Officer and as Officer in charge of the Graphics section. (U.S.A.F. Collection, Heritage Museum.)

Classroom Instruction. 1st Lt. Michael E. McCarthy and Capt. James M. Fitzsimmons review the T-38 flight plan. (U.S.A.F. Collection, Heritage Museum.)

Parade And Review. The Feb 5, 1966 Parade and Review UPI Class 66-E. Officers left to right are: Col. Chester Butcher, Col. Sherwood, Col. Franks, Col. White, Lt. Col Frantz, Lt. Col. Preston, Lt. Col. Wahl, and Maj. Butcher. (U.S.A.F. Collection, Heritage Museum.)

Inspection. General George Simler, Air Training Commander, is arriving at Webb AFB for inspection. (U.S.A.F. Collection, Heritage Museum.)

1968 Graduation. Gen. Dean speaks at podium at the student graduation of Class 68B. The instructors are seated at front table. (U.S.A.F. Collection, Heritage Museum.)

1965 Graduation. Students at Webb AFB were honored during a
ceremony in the summer of 1965. Pictured left to right,
bottom row: Major Glen Lingenfelter, Chief of Academics, 1st
Lt. William F. Wesson, Capt. James M. Fitzsimmons, 1st Lt.
John T. Slaughter, Capt. Paul M. Sullivan, Capt. James T.
McDaniel, Capt. Harley D. Henry, 1st Lt. Kenneth E. Keeler.
Back row: CWO4 Raymond A. Seger, 1st Lt. James E. Hedges,
Capt. Roy O. Linn, 1st Lt. Joseph T. Burley, 1st Lt. Michael
E. McCarthy, Capt. Niles A. Carter.
(U.S.A.F. Collection, Heritage Museum.)

1966 Graduation. In April 1966, the academic instructors pose
for a group photo during graduation ceremonies. Bottom row
left to right: 1st Lt. Edward M. Cook, Capt. James M.
Fitzsimmons, 1st Lt. David Kurshan, 1st Lt. Vernon D. Farmer,
Major Richard A. Gray, 1st Lt. Michael E. McCarthy, 1st Lt.
John T. Slaughter, Jr., CW04 Raymond A. Seger, 1st Lt. James
E. Hedges, Capt. Robert K. Wagner, Capt. Roy O. Linn, 1st lt.
Arthur E. Greiner, and 1st Lt. John T. Stull. (U.S.A.F.
Collection, Heritage Museum.)

Classroom Tour. Sixth grade students from Park Hill Elementary listen to Capt. Roy O. Linn as they tour the academic classrooms at Webb. (U.S.A.F. Collection, Heritage Museum.)

Reviewing Flight Plan. 1st Lt. James E. Hedges and 1st Lt. Joseph T. Burley review the T-37's flight plan. (U.S.A.F. Collection, Heritage Museum.)

Engineering. 1st Lt. Kenneth E. Keeler is being instructed on the T-37 engine. Engineering was a crucial part of pilot training and the student pilot had to be instructed on the mechanisms of a jet engine. (U.S.A.F. Collection, Heritage Museum.)

Weather Chart. CWO4 Raymond A. Seger and 1st Lt. Edward M. Cook look over the weather forecast chart. (U.S.A.F. Collection, Heritage Museum.)

Arrival of General Simler. On May 26, 1971, Col. Anderson W. Atkinson (left) welcomed the arrival of General Simler. Col. Atkinson served as Webb Air Force Base Commander from April 1, 1970 to July 31, 1971. (U.S.A.F. Collection, Heritage Museum.)

Class 68B. Left to right: Col. Sherwood, Col. Chester Butcher, and General Dean speak at the Class 68B graduation. (U.S.A.F. Collection, Heritage Museum.)

Former Wing Commanders. Five former Wing Commanders at Webb
A.F.B. gather for the 25th Anniversary of Webb in 1967. Left
to right: Col. Wilson Banks, Gen. A.F. Taute, Lt. Gen. Fred
Dean, Col. Ernest Wackwitz, and Col. Donald Eisenhart.
(U.S.A.F. Collection, Heritage Museum.)

Officers
Six Air Force officers stand in front of the Bi-centennial T-
38. Among the officers are Col. Stan Hanson, Col. Jerry
Grimes, and Col. Harry Spannus

Capt. Bennett. June 29, 1972, Capt. Steven L. Bennett and Capt. Mike Brown were in their OV-10 Bronco, piloted by Capt. Bennett, when they picked up a call from a South Vietnamese platoon that was in danger. Although the small aircraft only carried four small 7.62-mm machine guns and was virtually defenseless against enemy ground fire, the Captains joined battle. While under siege, a Soviet built SAM was launched from the ground and crippled Bennett's plane. Concerned with the safety of the South Vietnamese soldiers, Capt. Bennett limped his way to the sea. The SAM had shredded Captain Brown's parachute, making it impossible for him to eject. Capt. Bennett's chute was intact but he would not consider ejecting because it would mean certain death for his comrade. After plunging into the sea, Capt. Bennett was killed on impact but his heroic efforts saved the life of his partner Captain Brown, who was later rescued by Navy helicopter. (Prairie Pilot, Heritage Museum.)

Memorial. On August 8, 1975, a dedication ceremony was held to dedicate the new dining hall at Webb to Capt. Steven L. Bennett. Mrs. Bennett was also presented the Medal of Honor on behalf of her husband. She and her five-year-old daughter Angela stand in front of the commemorative memorial for Capt. Bennett. (U.S.A.F. Collection, Heritage Museum.)

Former Wing Commanders at Webb Air Force Base.

Col. Ernest F. Wackwitz
Oct 1, 1951 - July 16, 1953

Col. Fred M. Dean
July 19, 1953 - Nov. 20, 1954

Col. Charles M. Young
Jan. 10, 1955 - Aug. 6, 1957

Col. Kyle L. Riddle
Aug. 7, 1957 - Aug. 10, 1959

Col. Donald W. Eisenhart
Aug. 25, 1959 - Aug. 18, 1961

Col. Wilson H. Banks
Aug. 19, 1961 - July 8, 1963

B. Gen. Howard J. Withycombe
July 29, 1963 - July 5, 1964

Col. A.F. Taute
Feb. 1, 1964 - Dec. 6, 1965

B. Gen. Chester J. Butcher
Dec. 6, 1965 - April 15, 1968

Col. W.C. McGlothlin Jr.
April 16, 1968 - June 27, 1969

Col. H. Lobdell Jr.
June 27, 1969 - April 1, 1970

Col. Anderson W. Atkinson
April 1, 1970 - July 31, 1971

Col. Malcolm E. Ryan
July 31, 1971 - Aug. 6, 1972

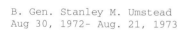

B. Gen. Stanley M. Umstead
Aug 30, 1972- Aug. 21, 1973

Col. Robert G. Liotta
Aug 21, 1973 - July 1974

Col. Robert G. Owen
July 1974 - June 1976

Col. Harry Spannus
June 1976 - June 1977

Preparing to fly:
In 1968, Major Jerry Grimes (left) prepares to fly a T-38
Talon with a civilian passenger, M.H. (Frog) Koger.

74

Four

Flying High

In 1967, Lt. Gen. Robert W. Harper, Commanding General of the
Air Training Command noted the Air Force had reached 95 combat
wings, with a goal of 120. He said "You can't fight
Communists with a feather duster."

Nature and Man. The strike power of nature and man is evident
during a lightening storm at Webb. (U.S.A.F. collection
Heritage Museum.)

T-38. Two T-38 trainers from Webb A.F.B., fly high above the clouds and over Big Spring, Texas. (U.S.A.F. Collection, Heritage Museum.)

Airship Formation. T-33s fly over Big Spring in airship formation during the 1950's. (U.S.A.F. Collection, Heritage Museum.)

Leaving New York. A/1C James E. Ranison gives, 1st Lt. Howard
Below, the wing emblem to take back to the new station in Big
Spring Texas. The Wing emblem was created during World War
II. The shield design is divided evenly with the colors blue
and red. The blue is to the left and denotes the freedom of
the skies. The red symbolizes the fire and blood of a world
steeped in war. The indented division of the melded colors on
the shield symbolizes striking power and quick action. After
arriving at Webb, the bottom insignia, "Above The Foe" was
replaced with 78th Flying Training Wing. (U.S.A.F.
Collection, Heritage Museum.)

Training in the T-41. Webb students began Primary Training in
the T-41 at Howard County Airport with civilian contractors.
(U.S.A.F. Collection, Heritage Museum.)

Star Fighter. Webb's single mission was to train jet pilots, but for a brief period of time it served as home of the 331st Fighter Interceptor Squadron, a component of the Air Defense Command. It arrived in 1958 from Stewart AFB, New York and remained until Dec. 2, 1967. It was responsible for intercepting unidentified aircraft in the southwest region. The F-104 Star Fighter was armed with lethal rockets and in 1962, was deployed to Florida during the Cuban crisis. (U.S.A.F. Collection, Heritage Museum.)

Huskie Helicopter. An HH-43F Huskie helicopter practices rescue operations. The giant blades of the crash rescue flier helped put out the flames in the event of a crash and ensuing fire. The helicopter could reach speeds of 120 miles per hour and could travel a range of 205 miles with a ceiling of 30,000 feet. (U.S.A.F. Collection, Heritage Museum.)

Parasailing. An unidentified flier parasails during a demonstration at the Bicentennial Open House. Parasailing and aircraft ejection procedures were part of the curriculum given to the training pilots at Webb. (U.S.A.F. Collection, Heritage Museum.)

T-38 Talon. These seven Northrop T-38 Talon jets make up the Thunderbird Fleet. The T-38 is a highly reliable aircraft and in 1976, it was the seventh type of jet flown by the team since it began flying with the F-84G in 1953. The Talon was specifically designed for training pilots. (U.S.A.F. Collection, Heritage Museum.)

Thunderbirds. Only a few feet separate each F100 flown by the
Thunderbirds. These supersonic fighter airplanes perform
during an air show. (U.S.A.F. Collection, Heritage Museum.)

Thunderbirds Demonstrate. The Thunderbirds Official Air Force
Precision Demonstration Team, lift their North American F-100
Super Sabers into the air. The team demonstrates the high
degree of coordination and teamwork required in modern
tactical jet flying. (U.S.A.F. Collection, Heritage Museum.)

Supersonic Jet. The T-38 is a
supersonic jet with flying
capabilities of 850 miles per
hour clip while soaring
55,000 feet high. These
T-38's are doing maneuver
s called 2-ship formation.
(Heritage Museum.)

Flight Panel. The flight panel
of a T-38. (Courtesy
of Peter Bird)

Rock and Roll. The T-38 was known for its high roll rate capability, achieving 720 degrees of roll per second. This view was taken by Peter Bird and shows the 'business end' of the T-38 in a 60 degree banked turn to the right. The "candy cane" in front of the plane, is the pitot boom. (Courtesy of Peter Bird.)

T-38's at Night. T-38 Talons are lined up on the flight line at Webb AFB. (Courtesy of Peter Bird.)

Bicentennial Talon. A T-37 and T-38 were ordered specially painted by Col. Harry Spannaus, in honor of the Bicentennial in 1976. (U.S.A.F. Collection, Heritage Museum.)

Pride Of 76. Master Sgt. Gilmore stands beside "Pride of 76 Howard County." (U.S.A.F. Collection, Heritage Museum.)

Pure Jet. A T-37 (Left) and a T-38 (right) were used in training the pilots at Webb. Once the program was changed to "pure jet", the T-37 was the main training aircraft. The UPT and Security Assistance Training Program students used it, and by 1975, Webb had eighty three T-38's in its possession. It was known throughout the Air Force as the "Tweet" or "Tweety Bird", and it would clock in at 400 miles per hour with a ceiling of 35,000 feet and a range of 650 miles. (U.S.A.F. Collection, Heritage Museum.)

Sky hawk Trainer. A Navy A-4 Skyhawk Trainer made a brief landing at Webb A.F.B. (U.S.A.F. Collection, Heritage Museum.)

Landing. Scenic Mountain provides a beautiful vista, as a T-38 Talon comes in for a landing at Webb Air Force Base. (Joe Pickle Collection, Heritage Museum.)

U.S.A.F. Fire Department. Webb's fire department was a branch of the Civil Engineering Division. They responded to fires in buildings and aircraft. The firefighting and rescue team worked within Webb and in cooperation with local fire departments during city and county emergencies. They were instrumental in fire prevention, fire safety and training. (U.S.A.F. Collection, Heritage Museum.)

Helicopter at Webb. A helicopter aids in a fire drill during a training exercise at Webb AFB.   (U.S.A.F. Collection, Heritage Museum.)

Maintenance Division. The maintenance division was responsible for the upkeep of the aircraft and aerospace equipment as well as the transient aircraft that landed at Webb for servicing. (U.S.A.F. Collection, Heritage Museum.)

Altitude Chamber. Another phase of student training required instruction in the "altitude chamber." The instructor (left) is teaching his student pilot (right) how to recognize hypoxia. The Sergeant at the control panel, simulates an altitude of 30,000 feet in the chamber. (U.S.A.F. Collection, Heritage Museum.)

Reviewing Flight Plan. Jets are lined up on the tarmac as two pilots review the pre-flight plan. (Worthy Collection, Heritage Museum.)

Five
Celebrating Freedom

Big Spring and Howard County enjoyed a close and friendly relationship with Webb AFB. Local business thanked Webb personnel for their patronage and support, while the entire city joined together to celebrate and congratulate Webb during its 25th birthday.

W.W. II Vets. A military band performs on the courthouse lawn during a Veterans Day Celebration honoring World War II vets. (Big Spring Herald Collection, Heritage Museum.)

General Wainwright. Lt. Gen. Jonathan Mayhew Wainwright IV
was welcomed to Big Spring by several local ladies as he
promoted his book, *Memoir, General Wainwright's Story.* Gen.
Wainwright was the senior field commander of the US and
Filipino forces under Douglas MacArthur. His Philippine
forces withdrew onto the Bataan Peninsula in early 1942, where
they occupied the entrance to Manila Bay. The defenders
earned the name "battling bastards of Bataan," as they
resisted Japanese attacks. The Japanese gained a foothold,
and Wainwright was forced to surrender the 3,500 men on the
island. Wainwright was held in prison camps in northern
Luzon, Formosa, and Manchuria until he was liberated by
Russian troops in August 1945. (Big Spring Herald Collection,
Heritage Museum.)

Veterans At Parade. World War II veterans are seated east of the courthouse and are watching Webb Air Force Base's 30th Anniversary Parade. The anniversary honored the Big Spring Bombardier School's beginning in 1942. (U.S.A.F. Collection, Heritage Museum.)

Pipe Band. The U.S.A.F. Pipe Band plays for the crowd during a student graduation at Webb. (U.S.A.F. Collection, Heritage Museum.)

Anniversary Coffee. In 1969, (left to right) Pat Pettigrew, Judy Francis, R.H. Weaver, and Col. McGlothlin join in the celebration of the Family Service's 12th Anniversary Coffee. (U.S.A.F. Collection, Heritage Museum.)

Color Guard. The Color Guard marches by the Settles Hotel, north on Runnel's street as T-37 and T-38 jet trainers pass overhead in formation. (U.S.A.F. Collection, Heritage Museum.)

Lackland Drum and Bugle Corps. Lackland Drum and Bugle Corps, play a spirited collection of marches as they march north on Runnels Street. (U.S.A.F. Collection, Heritage Museum.)

Gun Drill. A gun drill is being performed on Main Street during the parade. (U.S.A.F. Collection, Heritage Museum.)

Airman Caged. A float with an American airman in a bamboo cage, similar to those used by the Viet Cong, passed by the reviewing stand. Two men portraying Vietnamese guards guarded the airman. The message on the bottom of the float was, "Missing In Action, But Not Forgotten." (U.S.A.F. Collection, Heritage Museum.)

Parade Watch. The Settles Hotel towers over the large crowd as they gather on the corner of Main and Fourth Street to watch Webb's parade. (U.S.A.F. Collection, Heritage Museum.)

Col. Roy Ginder. Col. Roy Ginder leads airmen, in the parade, south on Main Street. (U.S.A.F. Collection, Heritage Museum.)

Women Marching. Women in the Air Force, (WAF) was established on June 12, 1948. Air Force women were trained, assigned, and administered under the same policies and procedures as the Air Force men. In 1972, 1,200 WAF officers and 10,000 enlisted women were in the Air Force, but no female pilot was ever trained at Webb. (U.S.A.F. Collection, Heritage Museum.)

Wagon Wheel Drive-In. During "R & R time," Webb airmen enjoyed the Wagon Wheel Drive-In, located at the corner of Birdwell Lane and Fourth Street. The drive- in allowed the customer to have their order delivered to their car by a carhop. While off duty, a pitcher of beer and frosty cold mugs was usually the order. (Heritage Museum.)

Jet Drive In. The Jet Drive-In was owned by the Robb family and was first constructed in 1952 at the end of Gregg Street. The drive-in theatre was demolished when the property was sold and became the Highland Shopping Center. Terrace Drive-In Theatre, also owned by the Robb family, was located on Wasson Road and renamed "Jet Drive-In". (Heritage Museum.)

Antique Airplanes. Wilson C. "Connie" Edwards, a Big Spring
rancher, gave visitors at Webb's open house a glimpse into the
past with five of his antique airplanes from World War II.
Shown left to right are: Col. Chester Butcher, Connie Edwards,
unknown and Lt. Gen. Sam Maddox. (U.S.A.F. Collection,
Heritage Museum.)